# MERELIZ COTTAGE GARDEN

## OR

## A GARDEN FIT FOR A COTTAGE

Elizabeth Reeve.  March 2013

To Mick

without whom Mereliz Cottage Garden would not exist

# CONTENTS

# Chapter 1

## Beginnings

It all began about twenty years ago, I suppose, the beginning of a dream which has now been a reality for half of that time. All those years ago, my mother mentioned that she was thinking of selling her terraced garage to the family next door. But this was no ordinary garage, it was a very old, possibly 17th century, one-up, one-down cottage next door but one to where I had been, not exactly born, as that had been in a nursing home, but brought up and lived until I married in 1965.

No. 4 Lower Sprotborough had been condemned in the mid 1950s as unfit for human habitation and the man living there had been moved into more suitable accommodation following the building of council houses which had taken place following WW2.

As a result of my objection to its sale, I later discovered that in April 1996 my mother had decided to gift it to me and, as she lived longer than the required seven years, it duly came into my ownership after that time. But she wasn't quite ready to give it up at that time and, as it happens, we didn't have the money needed to make it habitable either, so she continued to park her car in it until sometime during 1998, when, at the age of 84 and following operations on her hands for carpal tunnel syndrome, it was decided that perhaps she should give up driving. And so, in March 1999, plans were drawn and the renovation began.

Two or three eventful years later, which may in time be recounted elsewhere, on the 6th of December 2002 to be exact, our furniture arrived from store, we moved in and, before too long, began to think about the garden.

The front of the cottage is paved, with only a very small patch of soil remaining under the front window and two small diamond-shaped beds over which the car can be parked when necessary.

Mereliz Cottage

The main garden, then, is at the back, measuring approximately 35' wide by 50' long.  At that stage, it couldn't be called a garden, as during the renovation of the cottage, it had been covered by piles of old bricks, stone and miscellaneous junk surrounded by lots of increasingly pot-bound flowers and shrubs that we had bought, there being no visible soil in which to plant them. With the cottage renovation complete, what materials were still scattered around would be used to create the hard landscaping, and so we began to consider the design.

March 2004

Mick, my husband, had completed a Diploma in Horticulture following his redundancy from British Gas in 1995 and so was well able to take this on, but by this time we were working as camp-site managers in Lincolnshire during the summer season and so had to do as much as we could before starting work at the end of March. I had my own ideas about how I would like it, of course, but compromise was necessary if we were to get anywhere and we eventually came to a tentative agreement.

As will be understood by the measurements given, the garden is an oblong shape, bounded on the right-hand side by a stone wall. Across the top was a small building, divided into two, adjacent to the gable end of a stone building which belongs to the pub next door, and the left hand side was edged by an earthen path leading to the orchard of our next-door neighbour. The fourth side overlooked, as it still does, a drop of about eight feet into our back yard. As the garden is reached by two sets of steps, it could be described as a giant raised bed and, although it is on the north side of the cottage, because it is raised up, the sun, when it cares to, shines on some part of it most of the day.

The building described above, which had previously served the purpose of toilet and shed, had been in a state of terminal decay for some years so that it was now falling down with a tree growing in one side of it; we decided it all had to be removed. It would become the site of our 10' x 8' greenhouse, which had been Mick's 25 year service award from work, and a new shed, measuring 6' x 4', which, to the chagrin of Mick and much frustration ever since, was destined to hold the contents of the garage of our previous detached house which measured approximately 10' x 12'; the search for the simplest tool or device eliciting a loud clatter and a stream of barely contained abuse as said item would fall to the floor amidst a multitude of other implements, necessitating the removal of everything in sight to find it again.

From 1956, when my mother purchased the cottage, she had gardened it in a way that kept it tidy, with a few shrubs, perennial borders and a lawn. It had provided a drying space for her washing and each spring allowed free rein to many primroses and grape hyacinths which covered the large lawned area and the path border respectively. After she remarried on Boxing Day 1962, my step-father, Norman, planted vegetables: most successfully, runner beans which covered his wigwam frame in profusion each year, encouraged by the prior preparation they received in the form of manure from our bucket toilet which sometimes became full before the lorry arrived to empty it. Following his death, my mother returned to her earlier system, already having enough to cope with in the garden at her own home and the primroses and grape hyacinths continued to increase until they were covered over by our recycled 'junk'. This then was our inheritance and we set about our dig and design with enthusiasm.

The greenhouse and shed were to be separated from the rest of the garden with access being from the top of the path. Parallel to these structures, Mick built a stone wall, backed by a fence, on which to store wood for the fire and this was topped by a tiled roof, matching the roof of the cottage. A fence at right angles towards the gable end completed this space. The earthen path stretching the length of the garden would also be separated by a fence, and an archway leading onto the garden from the top of the steps, would create an enclosure both private and sheltered.

One of our firm decisions was that we didn't want a lawn, but we did want a rockery so, having dug the whole of the ground three times over and denuded it of as many weeds as we could find, we utilised some of the lumps of limestone still laying around, to build one on the edge overlooking the yard.

Fortunately, though time consuming, the digging wasn't too arduous as, with the addition of organic matter over many years, the natural texture of the soil makes quite a good growing medium. Bearing in mind that the underlying stratum is limestone, we have found that it is possible to grow a vast range of perennial plants, though acid soil lovers are not so happy unless in pots. The rockery was designed to cover an area of about 4' wide by 12' long, with a herb garden at the end near the steps and a planting area around two sides of the patio which we sited in the other corner. This corner actually overlooks our neighbour's back yard so needed the shelter of the Buddleia which remained as a legacy from the garden's earlier incarnation.

We also decided we would like a summerhouse and a water feature, so the top corners became homes for these. The water feature, raised up and fronted by a stone wall, with a ledge on top which can be used as a seat, backs onto the wood store and the summerhouse is such that its two back walls fit into the right-angled corner on the right. To facilitate access to these, we decided that the path should continue in a rectilinear route from the top of the steps, through the arch, along the front of the rockery to the patio, and then from the patio to the summerhouse where it again turns left towards the water feature. This had the advantage of creating a flower bed on the right and another on the top border, leaving a large area in the middle.

There are, however, disadvantages to this design which have become more apparent has time has gone on and plants have grown, in that it is constantly necessary to retrace one's steps to return to the archway and it can be very difficult to gain access to any plants which need attention in the large middle bed. But these weren't so apparent at the time and, having made the decision, we resolved to go ahead with this plan. The good thing about gardens, however, is that nothing has to remain static and ten years on we have already had to consider as well as implement other more unexpected changes.

But between March 2004 and Summer 2005 when the first plantings were becoming established, we were very pleased with our new garden and  looked forward to viewing and enjoying the fruits of our labour from the comfort of a deckchair.

Summer 2005

# Chapter 2

## Trees

In retrospect, I think we have been over-enthusiastic in our tree planting - well that probably applies to everything in our garden, but trees grow much bigger than perennials, don't they.

In 1997, we acquired a very small *Dracaena draco* or Dragon Tree in Gibraltar. Mick was doing work experience in the Alameda Botanical Gardens at the time and we carried it with us all the way round Europe before coming home. As it was tender, it had to be contained in a pot so that it could be brought inside for the winter so, fortunately, it grew very slowly as it lasted for about ten years and became quite heavy, but alas it did not survive.

At the present time we have seven trees, one of which, the Buddleja, is not strictly a tree, but as it grows to 10' or 11' high each year, I'm including it. As I said before, it has been in its present position for many years and, although they seem few and far between this year, butterflies are reputed to like them, so no doubt it will be staying. We do cut it well back each year, but despite this harsh treatment its beautifully perfumed, large purple blossoms never fail to arrive.

In February 2003, Mick bought me a *Salix caprea pendula* for my birthday. Better known as the Kilmarnock Willow, it is a weeping tree which has been top grafted onto a trunk. It started its time with us on the right border, but now stands on the edge of the rockery where it can be seen from our landing window. As the garden is raised up so high from ground level, this is the best way to get a good view of the whole garden and I often stand there watching the birds and wondering if something should be pruned back or removed entirely.

The Buddleja in 2005

In nine years, the Salix has reached a height of about 5' and throughout the summer its branches grow to almost touch the ground. But it's not well. We're not sure why, but last year, it developed rust on its leaves and, as it looked so unsightly, we decided to give it a total haircut in the hope that it would recover. I must say, it looked quite peculiar at the beginning of the year with its little stumps sticking out of the top and I thought we might have killed it off, but no, it has grown just as much this year. In the beginning, the new leaves were beautifully green, but as they began to drape down to the floor the rust appeared again. I have discovered by reading up on the internet that it is a problem that often affects the pussy willow and is caused by a variety of fungi and bacteria that can be deadly. As the solution can be time-consuming and not necessarily successful, perhaps it will have to go. If we decide on this drastic action, we may at least leave the trunk, suitably treated, so that we can grow something up it rather than having to dig out the roots.

in 2007

and with a cropped top in 2012

*Amelanchier lamarckii* was bought from the Horncastle Garden Centre in 2004 when we were working as campsite managers at Woodhall Spa in Lincolnshire and is planted in the right border not far from the patio. It is tall and still slender eight years later, its white blossom looking very pretty in the spring. Unfortunately this doesn't seem to last very long, though the leaves do provide good colour when they turn bright orange later in the year.

2007

and 2011

The *Corylus avellana 'Contorta'* or contorted hazel is both a blessing and a curse. Another Horncastle purchase in 2005, it really has pride of place in the large centre bed, which is rather unfortunate as the dark green leaves which cover it all summer are rather horrid. We tend to grow tall delphiniums or other sky-reaching plants in front to hide it, but it is redeemed in winter when its wonderful curly branches reach in all directions - and enhance indoor flower arrangements too.

in 2007

and 2012

In 2004, I decided I would like a fruit tree and we decided on *Prunus persica* '*Rochester*', a peach. It too is planted in the right-hand border, at the back of the patio and near the Amelanchier. The only peach that matured, untouched by grub or bird and beautifully formed, was ready for picking by the beginning of August 2008 and I hung a chiffon scarf in the tree to catch it in case it fell off. This was a good move, as I found it in the scarf the day before the judges from Doncaster in Bloom arrived, so I'm afraid we ate it there and then. It was delicious, beautiful white flesh and very juicy. The following year, we were blessed with more than twenty and looked forward to an ever-increasing crop in future years, but since then the fruit has either not set or small wizened examples have fallen off before ripening.

Harvest 2009

No doubt the changeable weather has had much to do with this. In addition, however, we have had leaf curl which isn't pretty. We normally treat the tree for this condition, but neglected to do so last winter, though I am led to believe that they don't like rain on them either and there is no way we can prevent that. Its position is not ideal either as its lower branches reach over the patio and interfere with anyone sitting there. So, do we cut our losses and get rid of it or should we show it some sympathy and give it another chance.

My favourite tree is the *Catalpa x erubescens 'Purpurea'*. This was also purchased in 2003, but didn't get into the ground until 2005, when it was still quite small. We were told when we bought it that it would be unlikely to flower for about eight years, but it has flowered since 2007 so perhaps that's a record. It stands in a small bed next to the water feature and, despite slight pruning last year, its tallest branches are now 16' or so. The book says it can grow to 50', but we are trying to keep it smallish so that we can enjoy the canopy.

It is a lovely tree with broad ovate leaves, about 10" long, which break as purple and then turn green. It also has the most beautiful white panicles of small flowers which are marked inside with a yellow and purple colour and stand up in the manner of those on the horse chestnut tree, though of a bigger and rounder dimension.

2005

*and 2012*

Another one bought in 2003, but not planted until 2005 is Viburnum opulus. Again, it could be a shrub as it has several 'stems' not really thick enough to call a trunk, but it is shaped like a tree and must be 10' or 12' high by now. It is sited in the centre bed across the path from the right-hand border and has lots of those lovely white snowball flowers in spring or early summer. Sadly, as it is the ornamental variety, it doesn't have the beautiful red berries that can be seen in the hedgerows in the autumn. I'm afraid I didn't realise this when we bought it, but it's too late now so we just get to enjoy the flowers which have multiplied year on year.

*2007*

and 2011

Because our garden is so small, we generally remove the lower branches of trees or reduce them to a minimum so that we can grow other things underneath, but I feel a nice tree adds that something extra to a garden - and the birds love them too.

# Chapter 3

## Hard-Landscaping

Hard-landscaping is the skeleton of a garden which is made beautiful by the addition of trees, shrubs and flowers.   When a piece of land is littered by piles of stone, brick and other rubble, most of which will be useful at some point, as ours was, it is hard to know where to start, but in 2003 it began to take shape.

Mick among the plants and a variety of building materials

But first, I must explain where all these materials came from. When we began the renovation of the cottage, the first thing we had to do was clear the back yard. The original cottage had a small back yard across which our right-hand neighbour had a right of way. Access from his yard was up some steps onto a raised path which either carried on past our left-hand neighbour or turned at right angles up our second set of steps to his orchard. There was a drop of two to three feet from this raised path into our yard and a stone wall, about 3' high from the back of the path held back our garden. Consequently, when our left-hand neighbour added a kitchen and bedroom onto his property, necessitating the removal of the back wall of his living room, my mother, in health and safety mode, agreed that all this stone could be dropped into her yard thereby saving anyone from falling into it from the path. So, after bricking up the back door to half its height, the yard had been filled in and topped with a concrete screed. Several skips were needed to remove this rubble, but the stone proved to be very useful.

We subsequently decided to enlarge the yard by removing the pathway and our neighbour's steps completely, allowing our neighbour to walk straight through from his yard to ours before going up new steps at the other end. This, however, created another difficulty, as when the path was removed, we discovered that the stone wall didn't go down to the ground.

Fortunately, our builder, with advice from his surveyor brother in Australia, was able to dismantle this wall and build a new one, with foundations sufficient to safely hold back six foot of earth, and drain holes to allow any excess water through. The result is a beautiful stone wall on which to hang a variety of plant holders.

More stone came from the back of our cottage, which was also removed when it was found to be unstable. But don't worry, it all worked out well in the end and we now have a new kitchen wall.

It was bad enough to start with, but then it just got worse!

We decided to begin in the garden with the rockery, partly because of the huge drop over its edge into the back yard and partly because we wanted something to look at and encourage us when we stepped out of the back door.    After digging it over several times, we eventually reached the stage of placing the stones and starting a little planting.

The rockery in June 2003 and June 2004

What a difference a year makes. By June 2004, not only was the rockery looking amazing, but the boundary of the garden was taking shape with fencing being erected.

During our renovation, the pub next door was building a new kitchen extension and presumably, because it was in the way, they decided to demolish a small building with a tiled roof which was adjacent to our side wall. We were quite shocked to arrive one day and discover them in the process of doing this, not only because it was a feature we liked, but because it contained an original two-seater toilet which, as the pub is a listed building we didn't think should have been removed. They also removed some lovely shrubs which had been growing in a small garden at the foot of the wall on their side, leaving us a view of extractor fans on the roof and an ugly fire escape.

The roof of the pub's old 2-seater toilet in 2002

As a result of complaining about all this, the brewery agreed to provide a fence which they thought they could place on top of our wall with short posts holding it up on our side. However, as the wall actually extended a long way down into the pub's yard, we felt the posts should be long enough to sink into the ground on their side and be bracketed so that they were more stable.  So, after yet more delay, they agreed to do this.

the new fencing in June 2004

The end result of this episode was that we were able to site our summer-house in the corner where the old toilet roof had been removed.

Summerhouse October 2004

2004 was a busy year for Mick. We were still working on the campsite in Lincolnshire and so apart from checking it over on days off, could only work on the garden between October and March but, by October 2004, the summerhouse was in place and the brick footpath up the side of the garden to our neighbour's orchard was well on its way to completion.

The earthen path leading to our neighbour's orchard in 2003 and the new herringbone design brick path taking shape in October 2004

With the brick path completed, the next step was to decide what to use for the patios and the main paths around the garden. As it happened, a solution was at hand because, in June 2004, we were lucky enough to acquire a load of York Stone paving slabs from my mother's ex-landlord for a very good price. I had lived at No. 1 Tower Cottages and No.2 was in the process of having a new floor. The floors of both cottages were stone slabs on earth, but these were being replaced with damp proofing and concrete. Due to her age, my mum's wasn't done until after her death in January 2005, but when the slabs of No. 2 were just left in the yard, we feared they might be stolen and so put in an offer which was accepted.

Some of the York Stone slabs purchased in June 2004

Once paid for, we needed to move them very quickly and fortunately our daughter arrived on holiday from the Isle of Man so she was commandeered to help. They were quite large and extremely heavy and it took us hours, but at the end of the day it was very satisfying to know that we had acquired a piece of history and that they would be just perfect for the job in hand.

By next spring, an archway and fencing along the left-hand side of the path had been erected. This was achieved partly in conjunction with the building of the water feature, again using rescued stone, as the fencing behind this feature had to sit on a stone wall which would accommodate the wood store.

Fencing in April 2005

The laying of the path was extremely arduous due to the weight of the slabs, but before they could be laid a foundation of limestone was put down. The slabs also had to be sorted for size and shape according to where they were to be placed and some also had to be cut to fit specific places. The job was interrupted one day when the cutting tool slipped and sliced into Mick's leg. Fortunately, it wasn't in a muscled area otherwise he could have bled to death, but, still, it was a lesson learned about the danger of the task in hand. A couple of steps were also needed to allow for the contours of the land, but it gradually took shape and looked very nice.

The path in April and the Summerhouse patio in May 2005

The stone boundary wall had been in poor shape for many years and we became concerned that if it wasn't pointed soon and subsequently collapsed it would be not only dangerous, but cause an enormous problem.  Although we only have the benefit of the top three feet or so of the wall, from the side of the neighbouring public house it must be at least twelve feet high.  Who would be responsible for the repair if it collapsed is a question I am unable to answer, but it holds back our garden and to see it descend into the pub's kitchen wouldn't be a very pretty sight.  So, the winter of 2006-7 was devoted to pointing our side.

Pointing the wall in March 2007

We also had a problem with the steps up to the garden.  Three steps lead from the back yard, but at a right angle to them are six more.  Our builder had put these in, but we found them very steep and narrow, making them particularly dangerous when wet and so it was decided to take them out and make the treads wider and rise shallower.  This alteration has proved a great improvement, both visually and in terms of health and safety.

During all the years this work was being undertaken, we were in dispute with the brewery about noise and odour pollution emanating from their kitchen. When it was planned to add the kitchen onto the side of the pub, we were assured that it would not cause any problems. However, as described above, our garden was adjacent to it and, part way through the build they hit a problem, with the result that its two gable ends were brought to within about two feet of the dividing wall instead of the original five or six. Fans, which had been built into the roofs facing each other in the gulley between the two gables, had proved to be very noisy and Mick had worn ear muffs throughout his work on the hard landscaping to overcome the din they made. There were also problems with the smell of food and smoke which would pour from the fans during cooking, especially if they burnt something.

The council's Environmental Health Officer was eventually persuaded to come and measure the noise levels and, after several visits, agreeing the decibel level was unacceptable, issued notices demanding a reduction in the noise. Some time later, the planning committee agreed that replacement fans could be fitted and, although they look like two spaceships, they are hidden by climbing plants and we can now hear ourselves speak.

Smoke from the pub's kitchen in May 2006

From the beginning of the renovation, I had wanted a weathercock and we had searched high and low for one that would be strong but would be in proportion to the position it would fill. I had scoured plant fairs, garden shows and the internet but most were insubstantial or much too big - probably suitable for a church tower or at least something very high up. And so it was with delight that I found just what I wanted in 2009. We were visiting our daughter who lives in Port Erin in the south of the Isle of Man and had decided to drive up to Jurby Junk, a massive place in the far north where they sell anything and everything. It was near there that we unexpectedly came across a garden centre and snapped up the weathercock of my dreams. It now stands proudly on the gable end overlooking the garden and is a fitting adjunct to the hard-landscaping.

# Chapter 4

## Planning and Design

During the first year of planting, I decided I would like to keep a record of everything we bought. I had never done anything like this before, so it took a while to decide how it should be done, but in the end I decided to use Microsoft Office Access. With this programme it is possible to make columns and insert data which can then be referenced according to each column.

The columns I decided on were:

Acquired/Planted: when, where from; how much paid came in later
Latin Name
Common English Name
Type: tree, shrub, perennial, etc
Site: where planted
Season: when it flowered
Description: what it looked like, colour, etc
Flowered: if it actually flowered
Current Status/Action: whether it had survived, needed moving or removing

This programme enables me to list the plants in alphabetical order by 'name', but I can also show them in 'site' order or 'type' if I want to. It is quite a time-consuming process to maintain a list like this and inevitably some new plants get missed off and others appear in the garden as if from nowhere. I try to write down and photograph all the new ones we buy and then have a session entering them into the database at a later date. Then they often get planted before I know where, which can be a bit frustrating, but on the whole I find it quite a good system for keeping track of what we should have where.

I feel sure many people would think I was crazy doing this, and I do myself sometimes, but as we were starting from scratch, it seemed like a good idea at the time.

My list at 31 July 2005 had 352 plants on it, including trees, conifers, shrubs, perennials, bulbs, succulents, climbers, ramblers, alpines, herbs and grasses. Some of these we had brought from our previous garden, some had been rescued from before we started work on the new one, some had been given to us and others had been bought. There are now nearer the 500 mark.

Before I could 'site' the plants, it was necessary to divide the garden into sections and so, going anti-clockwise around the edges from the archway, there was the rockery, next to rockery, right-hand border, top border, next to the water feature and water feature, leaving the centre bed undivided. The latter was quite a large area, but these were early days and it wasn't until the following year that it was divided into A, B, C, D and E (see below).

As this was to be a cottage-style garden, we intended that most of the plants would be perennials and, as it was on limestone, we knew acid-loving plants were unlikely to do well in it. Further, we didn't want any lawned areas and we also needed to cover the fences, particularly those on the pub side, where its fans continued to belch out noise, fumes and smells. The fire escape, too, could be a nuisance as, being in a poor area for mobile phone signals, staff from the pub would overlook our garden as they made use of its height to make calls.

Taking all this into consideration, we set about buying and planting climbing plants.

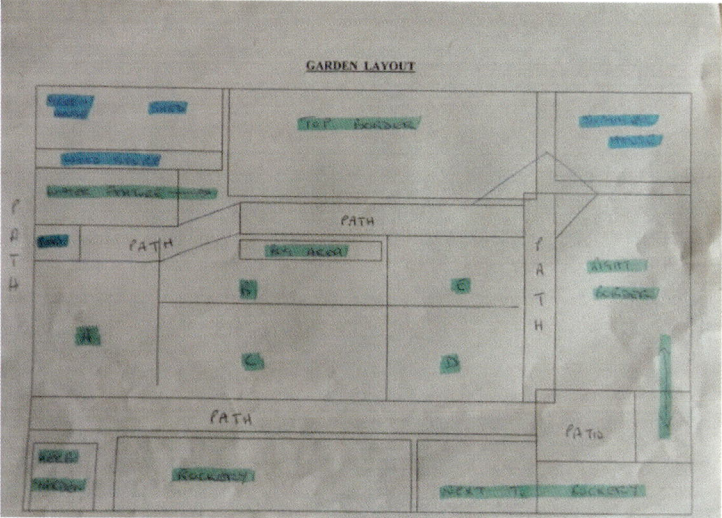

GARDEN LAYOUT

# Chapter 5

## Climbing Plants

One of the first climbers we put in, which soon fell by the wayside, was *Chaenomeles 'Madame Butterfly'* or Japanese Quince, which was a lovely salmon pink. There have been any number of plants which have gone the same way and it's difficult to know why beautiful, healthy-looking plants should suddenly wither and die. There could be many reasons, of course. We have the best and most athletic slugs and snails in the country which seem to eat anything and everything in sight, and we also have free draining soil, which can soon lose its moisture despite Mick's best efforts to bulk it up with organic material. Perhaps the soil is too alkaline for some plants. Whatever the reason, it is usually the most expensive which go first and I think we have now learned that cost is not always the best gauge of survival.

There are fourteen Clematis on my first list, but few of them could be described as vigorous. *C. 'Miss Bateman'*, *C. alpina 'Frankie'*, *C. 'Warszawska Nike'* and one other whose name I don't know, have come every year without fail.

C. 'Miss Bateman'

C. 'Warszawska Nike'

Some lasted for a while, but then disappeared, only to come again unexpectedly; C. 'Multi Blue' was one such which we had planted to go over the archway - but still it's been disappointing. C. 'Omishiro' and C. Piilu' are two more we bought at great expense, but again have not done as well as I had hoped. Even the evergreen varieties have failed to thrive, which should teach us something, but we seem to keep on trying.

One climber which we feared would take over the whole garden if we didn't do something about it was *Eccremocarpus scaber*, the Chilean Glory Vine. We planted it on the water feature and its bright orange blooms lived up to its glorious name. However, it produced so many seeds that we daren't leave it to do its worst and so removed it.

*Passiflora caerula*, the common passion flower also did well on the water feature. It came a cropper at pruning time but has recently been resurrected to grow up the fence on the side path adjoining our neighbour's garden.

Passiflora caerula

We also planted *Jasminum nudiflorum* on the water feature and its bright yellow flowers have continued to brighten that corner each year.

Two slightly more interesting climbers on the water feature were *Billardiera longifolia* with its purple fruit, which unfortunately seems to have disappeared this year, and *Akebia quinata*, the chocolate vine, which is now climbing high up into the Catalpa.

Akebia quinata

Billardiera longifolia

Several climbers were planted by the left-hand fence, including *Hydrangea petiolaris*, *Garrya eliptica* (the tassel tree) and *Vitis vinifera*, an ornamental vine which produces beautiful berries of many colours, from yellow to pink, to blue, to purple.

Hydrangea petiolaris

*Garrya eliptica with the tassels in flower*

*Vitis vinifera*

Roses have found their place too. The two planted on the front of the cottage were *Rosa 'Gloire de Dijon'*, a beautiful cream, and *Rosa 'Warm*

*Welcome'* which surrounds the door.

Rosa 'Warm Welcome'

This is a small-flowered rose, bright orange and lightly scented which everyone who arrives loves. The 'Gloire' however, turned brown when wet or dying and, as its flowers tended to hang on instead of dropping off, looked dreadful against the white render. It had to go and was replaced by *Rosa 'Masquerade'*. We had bought this for my mum one Mothering Sunday and rescued it from her back yard when she died. It has done very well since then and its blooms, which change from yellow to orange to pink, go well with 'Warm Welcome'. If the great flood in 2007 wasn't the best experience ever for us, at least 'Warm Welcome' benefited from the river giving it a good soaking and produced the most glorious, brilliantly orange flowers ever. Having a new front door, too, we painted it 'Heather' and bought *Rosa 'Rhapsody in Blue'* to match.

Rosa 'Rhapsody in Blue'

In the back, we have *Rosa 'Albertina'*, a cream with a beautiful perfume, over the arch, *Rosa 'Felicite Perpetue'*, a smaller cream, and *Rosa 'William Lobb'*, a purple, on the top gable, as well as *Rosa 'Arthur Bell'*, a yellow, in the top bed. 'Albertina' and 'Arthur Bell' were gifts which remind us of our time as camp site managers.

Rosa 'William Lobb

I should not forget, either, the pinky-red floribunda rose, a legacy from the old garden, which spreads its glory over a good part of the right-hand fence and onto the summerhouse for weeks.  I have no idea of its name, but it has been stunning every year and reminds us of the garden's previous life where runner beans, potatoes, primroses and grape hyacinths held sway.

The unknown floribunda rose

# Chapter 6

## Shrubs

I am aware that I have not always been totally accurate in my descriptions so far, in that some shrubs have been described as trees and others have been included in chapter 5 as climbers. The difference between a tree and a shrub is that whilst a tree has one main stem leading to branches, a shrub has several or many stems growing from the ground. The problem for me in describing those growing in my garden is that some of the shrubs, for instance the *Viburnum opulus*, has grown quite tall and so looks more like a tree than a shrub. Roses and honeysuckles, whilst being climbers, might also be considered to be shrubs. I do not profess to be an expert gardener, only a beginner, describing what I see, so, having admitted my failings, I hope I might be forgiven.

Although I hadn't realised how many, I discover in the course of this exercise that we have a great many shrubs, probably 45-50 not including those I have mentioned in previous chapters. The buddleia, hypericum and spiraea as well as the anonymous rose, with which I ended chapter 5, were all inherited, though the middle two have since been removed. The hypericum in particular seemed to be self-seeding in all the wrong places around the garden and had to go.

It is inevitable that some have been lost despite great efforts to keep them alive and others may have died due to adverse weather conditions having done well for a few years. Yet more may just have been too tender for our part of the country - not having space to store everything inside during the winter doesn't help. Despite this, we have managed to hold onto several Abutilons for quite a number of years which are cared for in the greenhouse in winter and brought out into pots each year.

In the first group can be placed *Camellia x williamsii 'Donation'.* which produced the occasional beautiful pink bloom, but really prefers acid soil and gradually faded away.

Camellia x williamsii 'Donation'

Hamamelis x intermedia 'Arnold Promise'

In the second, I would place *Lophomyrtis x ralphii 'Red Dragon'*, a beautiful little shrub, light and airy with dainty foliage which turned from a greeny orange to a reddish purple. This was the only one of five, bought with a gift voucher from our daughter in 2009, to succumb very quickly to frost.

The *Mahonia x media 'Charity'* and *Hamamelis x intermedia 'Arnold Promise'* are still growing nicely. The other two were the white *Hebe diosmifolia* and *Rhododendron impeditum 'Blue Steel'*, both dwarf varieties, the former living on the rockery and the latter in a pot because of its need for acid soil.

The most disappointing plant we have ever bought was the supposedly 'climbing' *Fuchsia 'Lady Boothby'* as it was the most expensive. I have to admit it looked very healthy when we bought it, but it produced very little new growth or flower during the year and then disappeared. We have certainly had many more fuchsias which have cost very little and been beautifully productive.

I see from my list that at least six of the nine shrubs purchased in 2003 are still doing well, the *Cotinus coggygria*, or smoke bush, is one and *Cornus alba 'Aurea'*, a dogwood is another.

Both of these were bought from Horncastle Garden Centre whilst we were campsite managers in Woodhall Spa and provide fantastic colour all year round.

The Cotinus with the Catalpa in the background

and the Cornus alongside the Buddleja

Another we bought in Horncastle was.   This was a complete experiment for us as we had no idea what it was or would turn out to be, but when it did bloom its flowers resembled the 'bottle brush' with sparkling racemes of crimson filaments and golden anthers.

Metrosideros tharcissi

A Cistus, a Lonicera and a Skimmia japonica have all weathered the harshest conditions we have experienced to date, as has the aptly named which produced masses of beautiful white flowers alongside  the path this year.

Exochorda x Macrantha 'The Bride'

In 2005, another ten or so arrived, my favourites being *Piptanthus nepalensis* and *Coronilla valentina ssp Glauca*. Both of these have yellow pea-like flowers and had been consistently good until a couple of years ago when the Coronilla died on us, probably due to that terrible winter. I was very sad about this as it flowered on and off throughout the year and had a lovely perfume. Unfortunately, they aren't seen in garden centres very often, so when we came across Coronilla citrina this year, I couldn't resist it.

Coronilla citrina

A variety of shrubs can be seen in the picture overleaf on the water feature, from the left: *Coronilla valentina, Exochorda x Macrantha 'The Bride', Piptanthus nepalensis* and, bottom right corner, a *Paeonia suffruticosa* (Tree Peony)

The *Choisya ternata* also suffered in the frost and had to be drastically cut back, but it is still managing to survive though in quite poor shape. *Sarcococca humilis* or Christmas Box is another that doesn't seem to want to live with us. The first is still struggling after seven years and the second, which we had in a pot at the back door in the hope of taking advantage of its winter scent, was frozen to death.

Choisya ternate

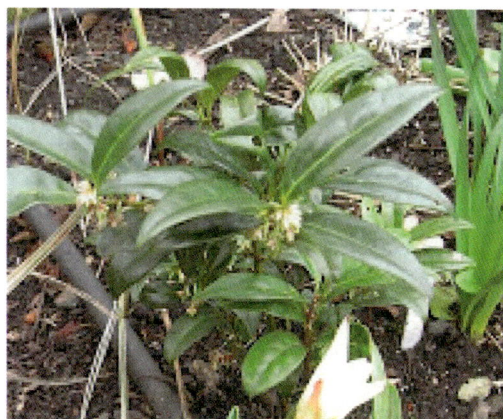

Sarcococca humilis

Shrubs which I think have some similarity in appearance, though being of different sizes are weigelas, deutzias and a lonicera. In our garden, they are all pink, the weigela being the largest at approximately five to six feet high with stems which are usually heavy with flower.

The next in size is one which is still to come into its own - the *Deutzia pulchra*. We have planted it on the water feature where the original Coronilla lived and I am waiting in anticipation for it to fulfil its early promise.

The next in size is the *Lonicera syringantha*, an airy, many stemmed shrub with tiny leaves and flowers which smell beautifully despite their size. This was one of three rescued from the 'sale' section of a garden centre at a very cheap price which have done well - the others being a *Berberis x stenophylla* which has brilliant yellow-orange flowers followed by blue/black berries and *Philadelphus 'Mont Blanc'*, a small-flowered mock orange.

To return to the deutzias, the smallest we have is *Deutzia x elegantissima 'Rosealind'*. Having been purchased in 2010, it is still quite a small plant, but has flowered profusely each year since then and the tiny star-shaped, pink-tinged white flowers are just beautiful.

Weigela

Lonicera syringantha

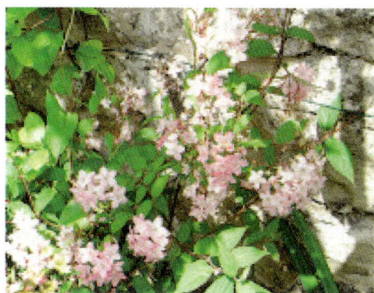

Deutzia x elegantissima 'Rosealind'

In 2007, fashion dictated that we should have some blueberries. As with rhododendrons and camellias, they like acid soil so there is no alternative but to grow them in pots. However, both *Vaccinium corymbosum 'Elizabeth'* and its companion, V.c. *'Darrow'*, have done well, producing a reasonable amount of fruit each year. This year has not been so good, but perhaps the rain has had something to do with that. This was also the year I threatened my *Syringa x laciniata* that if it didn't do better the next year it would have to go.

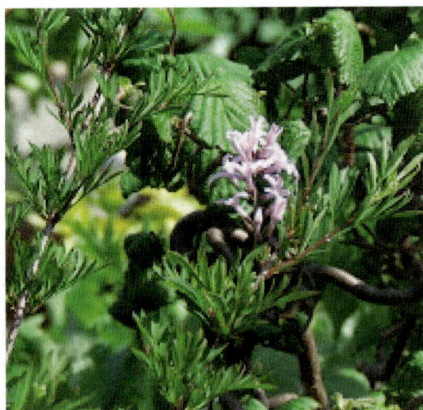

Syringa x laciniata

We had bought this shrub in 2003 with the expectation that its perfume would fill the garden, but in 2007 it produced its first - and last - flower, which was a shame as it seemed ideal size for a small garden, reaching about 4-5 foot in height and with a pretty flower and fine leaves. Needless to say 2008 was no better and it didn't get another chance.

This year, besides the Coronilla, we have added *Lonicera fragrantissima*, which is winter flowering and looks quite a beauty on the plant label, and *Viburnum sargentii 'Onondaga'*, the latter to replace the giant Yucca which I had grown to hate, but to which Mick was sentimentally attached as he had brought it from Gibraltar in 1997 as a two-inch baby. I am not sure what these two will turn out to be, but hope the winter is not so bad that they will be cut off before they have a chance to reach their prime.

*Lonicera fragrantissima*

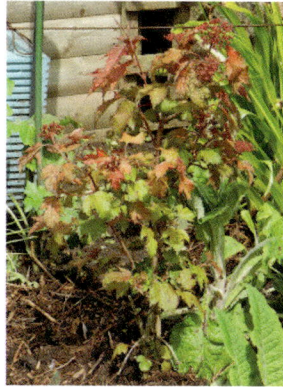

*Viburnum sargentii 'Onondaga'*

## SHRUB LIST

Abutilon
Berberis x stenophylla -
Buddleia Davidii
Camellia x williamsii 'Donation'
Ceanothis 'Yankie Point"
Choisya ternata, mexican orange blossom
Cistus x dansereaui 'Decumbens' (Rock Rose)
Coronilla valentina ssp Glauca
Coronilla citrina
Cotinus coggygria - smoke bush Cornus alba 'Aurea' dog wood
Daphne mezereum 'Alba'
Helianthemum  (Rock Rose - suitable for a rockery)
Deutzia x elegantissima 'Rosealind'
Deutzia pulchra
Exochorda x Macrantha 'The Bride'
Fuchsia 'Lady Boothby'
Garrya eliptica
Gaultheria procumbens
Genista
Hamamelis x intermedia 'Arnold Promise' (Witch Hazel)
Hebe diosmifolia
Hebe macrocarpa 'Margret'
Hypericum
Kerria japonica (Jews Mallow)
Lonicera syringantha
Lonicera fragrantissima  (honeysuckle)
Lophomyrtis x ralphii 'Red Dragon'
Mahonia x media 'Charity'
Metrosideros tharcissi
Paeonia suffruticosa  (Tree Peony)
Philadelphus 'Mont Blanc' - mock orange
Piptanthus nepalensis
Pyracantha 'Orange Glow'

*Rhododendron impeditum 'Blue Steel'*
*Roses*
*Santolina rosmarinifolia*
*Sarcococca humilis (Christmas (or Sweet) Box)*
*Skimmia japonica 'Rubella'*
*Spiraea japonica 'Alba'*
*Syringa x laciniata (lilac)*
*Vaccinium corymbosum 'Elizabeth'*
*Vaccinium corymbosum 'Darrow'*
*Viburnum opulus*
*Viburnum sargentii 'Onondaga'*
*Viburnum x bodnantense 'Dawn'*
*Weigela*

# Chapter 7

## Winter: December to February

Considering that this literary enterprise has progressed in a timeline from 'beginnings', through 'trees', 'hard landscaping', 'planning and design', 'climbers' and 'shrubs', it would seem logical to write about perennials in this chapter, but there are so many perennials, and we seem to have bought most of them (just joking, but that's what it seems like), that it could turn into the RHS Plant Finder. So, having thought about it, I have decided to go through the seasons, starting with Winter, which I am classing as from the beginning of December to the end of February.

Beginning to write this chapter on the last day of 2012, I can tell you that I have today photographed the following plants which are presently in flower:

*Coronilla citrina*
*Corylus avellana 'Contorta' catkins*
*Cyclamen*
*Daphne mezereum 'Alba'*
*Erigeron karvinskianus 'Profusion' (Mexican Daisy)*
*Garrya eliptica*
*Graptapetalum paraguayense*
*Hamamelis x intermedia 'Arnold Promise'*
*Lycesteria formosa*
*Mahonia x media 'Charity'*
*Rosa (Patio)*
*Primula vulgaris (Primrose)*
*Rhodochiton atrosanguineas*
*Rosa 'Rhapsody in Blue'*
*Sarcococca humilis*
*Winter Jasmin*
*Viburnum x bodnantense 'Dawn'*

Most, like the Corylus, Daphne, Garrya, Hamamelis, Jasmine, Mahonia and Sarcococca were specifically purchased as winter-flowering plants so are not unusual. Likewise the cyclamen and primrose, though the latter seems a little early.

Daphne mezereum 'Alba'

Garrya eliptica

*Mahonia x media 'Charity'*

Others are just hanging on from Autumn, for example the Lycesteria and Mexican Daisy, but the rest are more of a surprise. The roses are making new buds, though are likely to be bitten back with the arrival of harder frosts.

*Graptapetalum paraguayense* is a succulent, described in the RHS 'Garden Plants' as frost tender. It was given to us by a friend in France, but it survived the harshest winter we have had for some years in 2011 and is still hanging in a basket on the front of our cottage. It is not in flower, but I feel that the fact that it is surviving deserves a mention.

*Mexican Daisy and Graptapetalum paraguayense*

The climbing plant, *Rhodochiton atrosanguineas*, which sports solitary tubular flowers and pretty delicate pink, bell-shaped calyces was bought as an annual at a charity event in late Summer with the expectation that it would only last into the Autumn, but it too has survived a frost or two and is still flowering.

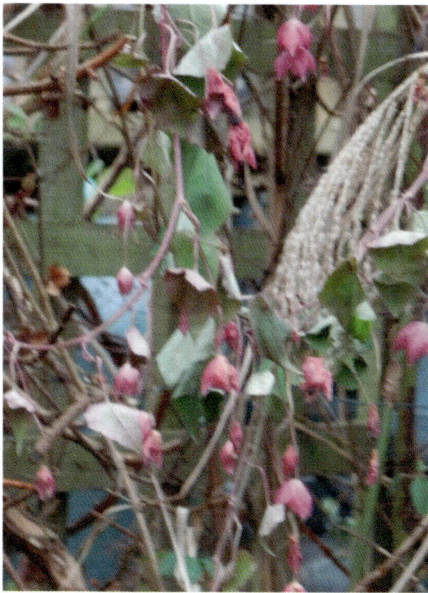

Rhodochiton atrosanguineas

A few weeks ago, we had some very hard frosts and some of the plants created quite an impression, but the recent wet weather has made it impossible to do any clearing up and the garden now looks very bedraggled.

Frosted Teazles

Everywhere is covered in leaves and the seed-heads left for the birds are, on the whole, broken down and rather sad looking. However, having passed the shortest day on the 21st December, we now look forward to brighter, and hopefully drier, days ahead.

Looking through my catalogue of plants acquired since the garden was started, I find there are few to add to the above and those are still to appear. Crocuses, hyacinths, irises will arrive in due course, as will the hellebores, lasting well into Spring. Snowdrops should be some of the first. We bought three different varieties in 2009: *Ikariae 'Woronowii'*, *'Elwesii'* and *Nivali 'Flore Pleno'*, but I don't know where we planted them so am hardly likely to recognise them when they arrive. No matter, I know they will look lovely. Last year our lane was inundated with them and we hope for the same again in 2013.

Snowdrops at Lower Sprotborough overlooking Sprotborough Flash

It is now the middle of January with frost on the ground and snow flakes drifting gently down and the question to be asked is whether we have found somewhere inside for all the tender plants or whether we will find come Spring that we have missed and, consequently, lost something. Whatever the truth of this, the greenhouse is full, as is the summer house. The latter has recently been divested of a mouse's nest, the household of which would no doubt have devastated the plants stored there if not found in time, so hopefully that has been avoided. Only time will tell.

One of the delights of the winter garden is the variety of wildlife, particularly the birds which can now be observed more easily. With the trees, shrubs and plants divested of their leaves, they can be seen darting hither and thither or pottering around on the ground looking for anything tasty they can find. We have an abundance of Tits: Blue, Great, Coal, the occasional Marsh and Long-tailed, though the latter seem few and far between. Goldfinches come daily and a Nuthatch has suddenly become a more regular visitor. The occasional Thrush, Robins, Chaffinches, Blackbirds, Wrens and Dunnocks are ground feeders seen on a regular basis. Sparrows, however, are non-existent and have been missed for a number of years now, though a Sparrow Hawk has been seen.

Goldfinches

Nuthatch

Robin

Magpies are also around and Pigeons live in nearby trees, but thankfully are not a nuisance in the garden.  Squirrels and other wildlife come to steal the nuts, too, but our most prized creature is the grass snake who lays her eggs in our compost heap on a yearly basis, the young then being found all over the place in late Summer.

A cheeky Squirrel

Grass Snake

*A mouse takes advantage of the nuts*

A couple of winters ago, we had a very welcome flock of female pheasants, escorted by their brilliantly-coloured spouse, who arrived daily to wipe out much of the slug and snail population. Unfortunately, when breeding time arrived, they disappeared and the gardener's enemy returned. We have seen a few members of this species since, but not in such numbers nor on such a regular basis.

Dragon flies are also prevalent in summer; I believe the most common are Brown Hawkers which fly over in their thousands at a certain time in the summer, but we have also seen the male Migrant Hawker, a large beautiful blue specimen, on one occasion.

In the wider countryside, we know there are buzzards in the now disused local quarry, woodpeckers and jays, as well as herons and gulls and various types of water fowl on the nearby nature reserve. Great excitement brought twitchers that came to see the Little Egret and an Osprey when they made rare visits.

But on cold and frosty days in January, there is little one can do except walk around the garden and take pleasure in the plants which bloom during such times and happily share their fragrance with all who pass their way.

# Chapter 8

## Spring: March to May

We don't usually clear the garden at the end of the year, but leave the seed heads for the birds, which means that we look forward to some good days from February onwards when we can begin the clear-up operation. It's always a thrill when the winter begins to fade away, the green shoots push their way through the brown earth and we can begin to look forward to the wonders of the year ahead.

The first flowers to show their faces are usually primroses.

Primula vulgaris

Since we began the garden, we have been inundated with them. They covered the original lawn each spring and are still rampant in our neighbour's orchard. We don't have quite so many now as we have dug them up to sell at the annual plant sale of the Yorkshire Group of the Cottage Garden Society, but they must love the limestone subsoil and so continue to self-propagate and give us a wonderful show each year. The ubiquitous Spanish Bluebell is also impossible to root out. I would prefer to have the English variety, which does bloom in the nearby woods, but we seem to be stuck with the larger, stronger Spanish invader.

Hellebores are also wonderful self-seeders so that we never know where they will come up next. We now have several varieties, mainly the H. orientalis group, but also the *H. niger*, the smelly *H. foetidus* and a pretty pink *H. Hillier 'Hybrid's Double'* which is quite fragile in comparison with the others.

Helleborus Hillier 'Hybrid's Double'

Helleborus niger

The windflower, *Anemone nemerosa 'Vestal'* or *A. blanda 'White Splendour'* are also delightful accompaniments to the miniature tulips and daffodils which are available now and can be planted together in pots to make a lovely display. *Ipheion 'Album'* also makes a good companion to these as do the many Narcissus varieties, such as *N. 'Avelanche'*, *N. 'Bridal Crown'* or *N. 'Tete a tete'*.

Anemone - Windflower

Narcissus Triandrus Thalia

The larger varieties of daffodil and tulips aren't forgotten either and we have had exceptional value from *T. fosteriano 'Purissima'*, a fabulous white, and *T.triumph 'Negrita'*, an equally good purple, over a number of years. However, *T. double late 'Angelique'*, which was wonderful the first year, has diminished in quality and quantity since they were first enjoyed so much.

*Tulipa fosteriana 'Purissima'*

*Tulipa triumph 'Negrita'*

Rockery plants such as *Doronicum 'Goldcut'*, with its lovely bright daisy-like flowers add a touch of sunlight on dull days, as do the aptly-named *Lithodora diffusa 'Heavenly Blue'* and *L. 'Star'*. The Saxifrage family also come to life during this period and the ornamental strawberry, *Fragaria 'Ruby'*, will also be showing its pretty pink flowers and may even produce some fruit later on. The pasque flower, *Pulsatilla 'Alba'* and its blue equivalent also find themselves on our rockery and are beautiful reminders of the Easter story, with feathery seed heads left behind when the flowers are over.

Doronicum 'Goldcut'

Lithodora diffusum 'Heavenly Blue'

Fragaria 'Ruby

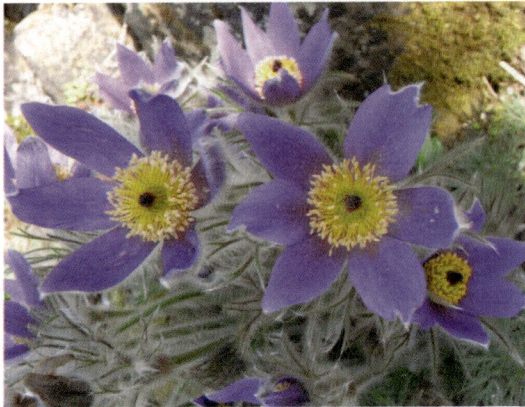

Pulsatilla vulgaris – Pasque Flower

*Fritillaria meleagris* is another woodland plant which grows well in our garden and has increased in number each year; both the white and the chequered varieties enhance the water feature, along with miniature irises and blue and yellow crocuses which the blackbirds seem to annihilate.

Fritillaria meleagris

Poppies are great, lifting their large colourful heads to the sky at the last minute. We had hundreds of them come up unexpectedly in the early years and assume the seeds had been in my mother's old compost heap. Needless to say, we had to go round pulling lots of them up, but we have since planted more specialised varieties, such as *P. 'Ladybird'* and *P. 'Curlilocks'*, as well as the smaller *Papaver nudicaule 'Pacino'*, the iceland poppy, which is so pretty and continues well into the summer and autumn.

Papaver commutatum 'Ladybird'

Papaver orientalis

Papaver 'Curlilocks'

We also have a well-travelled dark red peony which came to us via an aunt in London and my mother about 50 years ago. It then moved to Derbyshire with us and finally came back to Sprotborough ten years ago. Our daughter also took a a piece to the Isle of Man, where it continues to thrive, so it obviously travels well.

Peony

The *Persicaria bistorta 'Superba'* can be found at the back of the top border, but I particularly like the smaller, low-spreading *P. vaccinifolium* with its bright rose-pink spikes which flower right through the year and can even look good in their autumn colours until the end of November.

We did have the even smaller variety, P. 'Needham's Form', which has very small round pink flowers, but I'm afraid we lost it some time ago and it doesn't seem to be widely available.

I also have a small collection of *Primula auriculas* for which Mick built a 'theatre', but I'm sorry to say they haven't done as well as I would have liked and I have lost quite a number. Perhaps the position isn't quite right.

Ornamental grasses also begin to show the promise which will come to full fruition later in the year. The tall ones mix so well with later-flowering perennials, but the low-growing black grass, *Ophiopogon planiscapus 'Nigrescens'*, with its tiny blue flowers and black seeds is good value, multiplying whilst still being controllable. It is planted in the small plot at the front of the cottage which faces south and so gets lots of sun, but the floods of June 2007 did it no harm at all.

*Carex comans 'Frosted Curl' and Ophiopogon planiscapus 'Nigrescens' sit side by side at the front door*

A very unusual plant which I have only ever seen in one other garden is the *Haquetia epipachtis*, which has grown slowly into a small mound.

*Haquetia epipachtis*

I think it might be considered to be one of the few 'green' flowers, though they are relieved by yellow centres.

It would be possible to go on and on, but I will end by just mentioning three very different 'Vs': the lovely little violets, which also grow wild around here, *Veronica gentianoides*, with its graceful pale blue spikes, and *Vinca minor variegata*, a bit of a thug  which will take over if it's not kept under control.

Violets

Veronica gentianoides

The presence of these, along with shrubs and trees, which are now coming into flower or putting on leaf, are an indication that the spring garden is looking forward to a promising summer ahead.

# Chapter 9

## Summer: June to August

Views of the garden from the upstairs window of the cottage

The Spring Bank Holiday and early June herald the beginning of summer.
Frosts can be forgotten, bedding plants can be brought out into the garden
from the greenhouse or cold frame where they have been hardening off
and the roses begin to bloom in earnest.   Or at least they do in our garden.
Rosa 'Albertina' on the archway and Rosa 'Felicite Perpetue' on the top
wall, both pinky cream, but the latter much smaller, fill their allotted places
beautifully.  The other roses are not so prolific, though 'William Lobb' is
improving as the years go by.   But summer is the time for perennials and
there are so many to choose from.

Rosa 'Albertina'

Rosa Felicite 'Perpetue'

Rosa 'William Lobb'

## The Top Border

Framed between the shed and the Summerhouse, this area is backed by the purple *Cotinus coggygria*, *'Felicite Perpetue'* and *'William Lobb'*, but features several clematis as well as tall perennials such as Hollyhock; Allium; Astrantia and a yellow Verbascum.

The next layer, height-wise, includes such things as a peony; Smilacina, the false Soloman's Seal; Heuchera; Tiarella; Papaver 'Orientalis' and, one of my favourites, *Chaerophyllum hirsutum 'Roseum'*, a mauve cow parsley, which seems to be a rarity in our area, but is an excellent filler which spreads and sends its inflorescences just where they are needed, whilst not being a thug.

Smaller plants come in the form of primulas.

Astrantia

Chaerophyllum hirsutum 'Roseum'

Hollyhock

The Right Border

The floribunda rose with, in front of it, the Yucca which we removed in 2012

This border is backed by the unknown pink floribunda rose, which spreads across the roof of the summerhouse; ivy, various clematis, a *Ribes Speciosum*, and a couple of honeysuckles with foxgloves, *Veronicastrum virginicum 'Alba'* and several salvias making their way towards the front.

We have developed a special interest in salvias since our discovery of the vast range available. On our Year on the Road in Europe from September 1996 to September 1997, Mick worked for two weeks in La Mortola, the garden on the Mediterranean border of France and Italy, originally belonging to the Hanbury Pharmaceutical family who donated the land for RHS Wisley. Until that time, the only salvia we knew of was the bright red annual which is used extensively in displays in parks, but the gardener there staggered us by introducing us to over 200 varieties. Unfortunately, many of the most attractive are tender, which we have learned to our cost, and there are many deletions in my database. It is important when buying them, therefore, to check this out if winter storage is a problem. However, some are hardy and we manage to keep several going from year to year, particularly *S. 'Glutinosa'*, a pale yellow; *S. forsskaolii*, a purple with a white stripe; *S. mycrophylla 'Hot Lips'*, a white with a red tip; and *S. sclarea 'Turkistanica'*, pink to purple/white. Despite our losses, we continue to be tempted and a couple bought last year are still unknown quantities in the survival field!

Some of the salvias we have loved and lost:

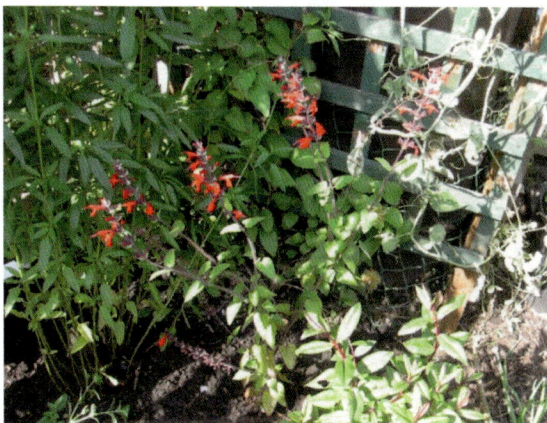

Salvia coccinea 'Lady in Red'

Salvia gesneriifolium

Salvia 'Indigo Spires'

Salvia uliginosa

Following the removal of the enormous Yucca from the top of this border, its space was filled with a *Viburnum sargentii 'Onondaga'* so that the Crinum Lily and Geranium should now be seen to better advantage.

Penstemon and Knautia

Bronze Fennel stands at each end of the border with a Bamboo in the centre and the burgundy-coloured *Knautia macedonica* mingles with lavender at the end near the patio. *Deutzia x elegantissima 'Rosealind'*, a small variety with the prettiest pale pink star-shaped flowers continues behind the table and chairs, alongside a heuchera, day lilies and *Echinops ritro 'Veitch's Blue'* which is really in the wrong place as it's spiky balls and leaves have to be fastened well back to protect visitors to the patio.

## Next to the Rockery

This area is an effort at a hot border, with *Crocosmia 'Lucifer'* and *Potentilla 'Monarch's Velvet*, though it does have the purple Buddleia at one end and the likes of *Aconitum carmichaelii 'Arendsii'*, *Ajuga reptans 'Multicolour'*, *Trycirtis hirta* - the purple toad lily, and yellow *Lysimachia punctata* at the other.  However, the pink version of *Rogersia aesculifolia*, *Skimmia japonica*, and red Monardas, Penstemons and Dahlias were planted there last year. *Rosa glauca 'Pourr'* also stands in a pot on the patio in the hope that it will add its tones to the array.

Crocosmia 'Lucifer'

You may remember from Chapter 2 that we were in two minds about the *Salix caprea 'Pendula'* which lived next to the rockery.  As it had developed rust and showed no sign of recovery, I can now report that it was removed.

## The Rockery

 Many of the plants here have been and gone by the time June arrives, but
nevertheless there are usually quite a number of small plants which carry
on flowering for a while longer.  There are also the *Geranium hymalayensis*
*'Flore Plena'* with its lovely double purple flowers, and the pale pink *G.*
*'Endressii'* , the old favourite, London Pride and *Fragaria 'Ruby'* , the pretty
ornamental strawberry which spreads by its runners, but is easily
controllable.   Lilies of the valley, and *Euphorbia cyparissias 'Red Devil'* -
both real thugs - also grow well here, but have to be pulled out at regular
intervals to reduce their hold.

Convallaria majalis - Lily of the valley

Ajuga reptans 'Multicolor' and Euphorbia cyparissias 'Red Devil'

The rockery is finished off at the end by what was supposed to be the herb garden with a Bay tree in the centre. The Bay Tree has survived well, but lavender has now replaced the herbs within the sections, which were created by box hedging, as it was found difficult to access them, sited as the garden is on top of the wall and at the side of quite steep steps. Hopefully the lavender will survive the winter.

## The Water Feature

Spring-flowering shrubs are in the majority in this corner, so when the Spring bulbs have finished, there is not a great deal to provide colour, but on one side is the *Deutzia pulchra*, a larger version of the *D. x elegantissima* 'Rosealind', which should flower in June; it is relatively young, but I am hoping it will have grown enough by this year to put on a good show. On the opposite side is the Catalpa which is beautiful in summer and enhanced by other climbers. Beneath the Catalpa small cyclamen have been planted, but a Crocosmia, Penstemon and Lily add to the effect as summer advances.

The Catalpa flower

Crocosmia 'Emily McKenzie'

*Lilium longiflorum*

## The Centre Ground

This quite large area is full of all sorts of perennials, but is also home to shrubs and trees.  The Daphne and Hamamelis have finished flowering by this time, but the aptly-named *Viburnum opulus* is super with its white 'snowballs'.  The Corylus is a disappointment in summer, with its heavy, dark-green, crinkly leaves and we do our best to hide it behind delphiniums and other tall plants.

In my opinion, some work needs to be done in this area, with several large plants needing to be removed.  For instance, another yucca has outgrown its space and a tree peony adds nothing to the design.   However, discussions are yet to decide their ultimate fate and in the meantime there are many good things to see.  Tall grasses, such as *Miscanthus sinensis 'Silberfeder'* and *Molinia caerulea ssp arundinacea 'Windspiel'*,  and *Kitaibela vitifolia*, a very tall white flower with separated petals give some height and the large pink *Lamium orvala* provides a good clump of medium-sized flowers. Nepeta and several varieties of geranium are very showy and mix well with Love in a Mist and Origanum. Poppies, Penstemon, Phlox and Phlomis vie for space with Salvias, Sisyrinchium and Sidalcia.

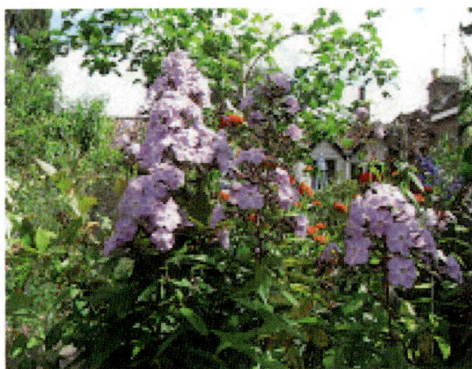

Phlox

The edges of the path are overlapped by Oxalis, Trifolium, Persicaria and Alchemilla Mollis, whilst seed from violets, aquilegia, poppies and many others force their way through cracks in the paving in an abundance of new growth.

Persicaria

Alchemilla Mollis

The cottage garden in summer is exuberant and colourful, bursting with vigour and vitality and only contained by stakes and rings and nets if they are put in at the right time in the right place.  If not, precious plants will almost certainly be dashed by the English rainstorm which 'came out of the blue' .

For those of us who love our gardens and want the best for them, someone has to spend many hours planning, propagating, pruning, preparing and composting before the flowers arrive, as well as watering  and dead-heading when they do.

To maintain a garden at its best throughout the summer is truly a labour of love.

The Courtyard Garden

# Chapter 10

## Autumn: September to November

SEASON of mists and mellow fruitfulness,
Close-bosom friend of the maturing sun;
Conspiring with him how to load and bless
With fruit the vines that round the thatch-eves run;
To bend with apples the moss'd cottage-trees,
And fill all fruit with ripeness to the core;
To swell the gourd, and plump the hazel shells
With a sweet kernel; to set budding more,
And still more, later flowers for the bees,
Until they think warm days will never cease,
For Summer has o'er-brimm'd their clammy cells.

John Keats's ode captures something of what can be expected during the months of Autumn, when gardeners awake to mists floating over their plots in the morning and welcome the fruits of their labours in the form of apples and pears and nuts and grapes if they are lucky enough to have space to grow them.

Unfortunately, our garden is rather small and the only fruit we have managed to produce so far are from two blueberry bushes which stand in pots on the patio, a few nuts on the Contorted Hazel and a good crop of peaches one year, seemingly never to be repeated again. Nevertheless, we enjoy this little excursion into 'fruitfulness' and take pleasure in the benefits.

I also have to admit that I am merely the supervisor who is mainly happy to oversee the labours of my husband in the collecting and drying of seeds, the taking of cuttings and the pruning of shrubs. This is not necessarily from choice, but because I am generally accused of going too far when I have a pair of secateurs in my hand! My forte seems to be in the clearing up afterwards arena; again, not necessarily my choice, but because I can't stand to see an untidy patch and can only restrain myself for so long. So I sweep the paths and the steps and remove the debris to the compost heap or the recycling bin.

September and October are often wonderful months and an Indian Summer might bring an extended flowering period for many perennials along with a second flowering of clematis and other shrubs, as can be seen from the photographs shown below.

Clematis tangutica

Alcea – Hollyhock

Sedum 'Ruby Mantle'

Salvia 'Wendy's Wish    '

Sanguisorba officionalis

Bronze Fennel

Fuschia

Knautia 'Melton Pastels' attracts a bee

Verbascum chaixii

But as the months pass and the fruit has been picked, the seed heads begin to form in readiness for collection for future years - or food for the birds throughout the winter. Late arriving butterflies and bees also take advantage of the nectar still to be had.

Despite the gradual dying back of the garden, however, unless the weather is so bad as to lay everything waste in one fell swoop, November too can still provide something to admire until winter arrives in earnest, when we begin to look for those really hardy plants which then come into their own.

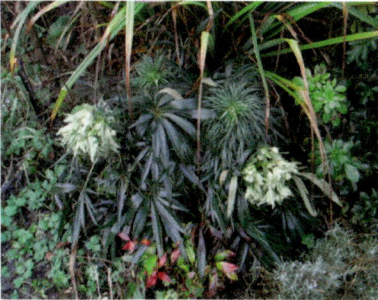

Hellibore foetidus or Stinking Hellibore

Viburnum x bodnantense 'Dawn'

November sunshine

Early frosts can provide quite a spectacle too, with sparkling plants and glistening spiders' webs, whilst a surprise fall of snow might suddenly clothe everything in white.

Frosted Grass

A pheasant in the pussy willow

Snow in the Courtyard

And so the seasons have come full circle and winter beckons once more. One more year has passed and we reflect on what has worked well for us and what we might need or like to change.

Unfortunately, we were unable to take part in Doncaster in Bloom during 2012 due to unforeseen circumstances, but we look forward to having another go at repeating previous Gold and Silver Gilt awards in 2013.

So, this is the end. I hope you have enjoyed reading about our garden in South Yorkshire and should you be coming our way and like to visit us, we would be happy to see you. Just send us an email and we will get back to you to arrange it.

Email: lizreeve17@gmail.com

The Author with her Husband, Mick

## Further reading:

Liz has published two other autobiographical books on Kindle:

'A Year on the Road', is a small book of theological reflections written whilst touring Europe in a motorhome whilst Mick did a year's work experience in chateau and botanical gardens for his Diploma in Horticulture.

'Two Lives' describes her evolving relationship with a drug-addicted son and her own religious life.

She is currently writing about the original renovation of Mereliz Cottage and subsequent flooding in June 2007 which necessitated doing much of the work again.

23421636R00061

Made in the USA
Charleston, SC
22 October 2013